MODERN ITALIAN COOKERY

ROZ DENNY

MARTIN BOOKS

THE AUTHOR
Roz Denny is a freelance cookery consultant and writer. She contributes
regularly to magazines, and is the author of several other recipe books.

Published by Martin Books
a division of Woodhead-Faulkner (Publishers) Limited
Simon & Schuster International Group
Fitzwilliam House 32 Trumpington Street
Cambridge CB2 1QY

First published 1988
© Woodhead-Faulkner Ltd

ISBN 0 85941 455 8

Design: Carrods Graphic Design, Cambridge
Photography: Eric Carter
Food preparation for photography: Roz Denny
Tiles on front cover and pages 41, 61 and 81 from Elon Tiles
Limited, London W11
The white china and cutlery on front cover and pages 9, 20/21,
64/65, 85 and 92/93 from La Porcellana Limited (Personalised
Tableware), London SW2
Typesetting by Goodfellow & Egan Ltd, Cambridge
Printed and bound in Spain by Cayfosa, Barcelona

CONTENTS

INTRODUCTION

There can be very few people in Britain today whose appetites are not whetted by Italian food. So many great dishes have become part of our daily fare – minestrone, spaghetti bolognese, pizzas, antipasto, macaroni, not to mention the wonderful ice creams and water ices. Yet there are many other Italian dishes, both traditional and modern, still waiting to be discovered over here. Not only are they truly delicious, but also really quite easy to recreate in our own kitchens.

The Italians claim to have been the creators of good Western food. Italian chefs arrived at the court of the French kings in the sixteenth century with the young Catherine de Medici, and there introduced a new style of cuisine, from which blossomed the classic French tradition.

But the real joy of Italian food lies in the simplicity of cooking methods, food textures and flavours. It uses excellent, inexpensive ingredients that need little extra attention – olive oil, pasta, cheeses and tomatoes. Italian food is perhaps one of the easiest to master because there are few complicated techniques. Free from the worry of possible failure, you can cook with much more enjoyment – in fact, Italian-style cookery is great fun!

TODAY'S HEALTHY FOOD

We are all being made aware of the benefits of a healthier diet. Most nutritionists now uphold the Italian Mediterranean diet to be one of the healthiest in the world: it is high in protein and fibre-rich grains, and low in saturated animal fats. Daily dishes revolve around pasta, cholesterol-free olive oil, tomatoes, pulses, medium-fat parmesan cheese, fresh fruit and vegetables, fish and light meats. If we were all to eat more like the Italians, then we would be heading towards a much better diet, and a more tasty and enjoyable one, too.

FOOD STYLE

Italy has only fairly recently, within the last century or so, thought of itself as one united country. Its history is one of several separate regions, and this is reflected in the glorious variety of regional dishes. A gastronomic tour from the richer north to the more arid south would reveal a gradual change from lighter, creamier food using more dairy produce, to a diet with more intense flavours and colours; where tomatoes and chillies are very popular, and even staple foods such as pasta are made without eggs, and dressed simply with oil.

Most ethnic or authentic foods from abroad often require unusual ingredients; not so with Italian foods. A quick glance at the recipes in this book will tell you that most of the ingredients they use are ones we tend to buy frequently anyway. So recreating a genuine Italian dish is not only possible, it's enjoyable and easy.

NAPOLINA PRODUCTS

Perhaps best known for its quality canned tomatoes, Napolina also makes an excellent range of authentic pastas, ready cooked pulses, parmesan cheese, tasty ready-to-serve pasta sauces and two grades of olive oil, including the best quality cold-pressed extra virgin oil, ideal for salads and special fried foods, and the pure olive oil, suitable for more general cooking and frying.

Napolina products are made in Italy from the very best ingredients. They are amongst the most authentic Italian foods you can buy, and, for many experienced cooks, synonymous with good taste and quality. That is why we say Napolina gives you a taste of the real Italy.

BUON APPETITO!

NOTES

Ingredients are given in both metric and imperial measures. Use either set of quantities but not a mixture of both in any one recipe.

All spoon measurements are level:
1 tablespoon=one 15 ml spoon
1 teaspoon=one 5 ml spoon

Eggs are standard size 3 unless otherwise stated.

1   SOUPS

The Italians are great soup-eaters, from a light soup to start a meal or clear the palate between courses, to a hearty main meal. Often the soups will be chunky, and served with extra grated cheese or maybe a spoonful of pesto stirred in. Most of these soups improve in flavour if made the day before required.

CHICKEN BROTH

Serves 6

1 onion, quartered
2 carrots, sliced
2 sticks celery, sliced
1 large leek, sliced
a small fresh chicken, or a large uncooked chicken carcass, or about 8 fresh chicken wings
2 bay leaves
bunch parsley stalks, tied together
150 ml (¼ pint) dry white wine, optional
2.25 litres (4 pints) cold water
salt and black peppercorns
grated parmesan cheese, to sprinkle

Put everything into a large saucepan. Cover with the cold water. Bring slowly to the boil, then cover and simmer gently for a good 1½ hours.

Strain, cool, then chill until required. The fat can then be spooned or strained off. For a more concentrated flavour, after removing the fat, re-boil uncovered until reduced by about half. To serve, boil up a handful of soup pasta in the broth and sprinkle on grated parmesan cheese.

Note: Broth can be stored in the fridge for a long time, as long as it is boiled up every 2 days for at least 5 minutes. It can also be frozen very successfully.

MIXED FISH SOUP

Serves 4

1 onion, chopped
2 cloves garlic, crushed
3 tablespoons extra virgin olive oil
150–300 ml (¼–½ pint) dry white wine
1.2 litre (2 pints) fish stock or water
2 × 400 g cans chopped or peeled plum tomatoes with herbs
pinch saffron strands soaked in 2 tablespoons hot water, optional

THE FISH
2 red mullets
750 g (1½ lb) mixed firm-fleshed fish, e.g., sea bass, monkfish or haddock
3 medium squid
12–16 mussels in shells
6–8 large Mediterranean or Dublin Bay prawns
4 tablespoons fresh chopped parsley
salt and ground black pepper

Sauté the onion and garlic in the oil for about 5 minutes until softened. Add the wine and simmer for 5 minutes to reduce down a little. Pour in the stock or water, tomatoes with herbs, saffron (if using) and seasoning. Bring to the boil, then cover and simmer for 20 minutes.

Meanwhile, clean and prepare the fish so they are free of scales and gutted. Cut into large bite-size pieces. Retain any heads which can be cooked in the soup (but remove before serving).

Pull the squid heads from the bodies; cut off the tentacles and reserve but discard the heads. Pull out the colourless bone and discard along with the insides. Peel the grey skin off, too, and discard. Wash the bodies very thoroughly, then cut into rings.

Scrub the mussels and wash the prawns. Lay all the fish on a large plate. When the soup liquor is ready, put the firm-fleshed fish in first. Simmer for 5 minutes, then add the mussels, prawns and squid. Simmer for a further 5 minutes. Sprinkle in the parsley, adjust the seasoning, and serve hot with crusty bread.

MINESTRONE

The best known and best loved of all Italian soups. Canned and packet versions bear very little resemblance to the real thing, which is very simple to make and extremely palatable. In summer, minestrone is also delicious served cold.

Serves 4

2 rashers unsmoked bacon, de-rinded and chopped, optional
1 large leek, sliced thinly
2 carrots, chopped
1 medium courgette, sliced thinly
125 g (4 oz) whole green beans, topped and halved
2 sticks of celery, sliced thinly
2 tablespoons olive oil
1.5 litres (2 ½ pints) stock or water
400 g can peeled plum tomatoes
1 tablespoon fresh chopped basil or ½ teaspoon dried basil
1 sprig fresh thyme, or good pinch of dried thyme
400 g can white or red kidney beans
50 g (2 oz) small soup pasta shapes or macaroni
salt and ground black pepper
grated parmesan cheese, to serve

Sweat the bacon, if using, leek, carrots, courgette, green beans and celery in the oil for about 10 minutes in a large covered saucepan. Add the stock, tomatoes (roughly chopped, if liked) herbs and seasoning. Bring to the boil, cover and simmer for 30 minutes.

Add the canned beans (with their liquor) and pasta, then simmer for a further 10 minutes. Serve hot, sprinkled with the cheese. This soup also improves if made the day before required, and can have a little pesto (see page 24) stirred in if you have any to spare.

Mixed Fish Soup; Minestrone

STRACCIATELLA

Serves 4

2 eggs, beaten

2 tablespoons grated parmesan cheese

1 tablespoon semolina

900 ml (1½ pints) good chicken broth (see page 6)

salt and ground black pepper

extra grated parmesan cheese and fresh chopped parsley, to sprinkle

Beat the eggs with the cheese, semolina and a cupful of cold broth. Put the rest of the broth on to boil. When just off the point of boiling, pour in the egg mixture in a slow steady stream. Wait a few seconds, then stir slowly. The egg should have set in small strands. Season, and serve immediately, sprinkled with the extra cheese and parsley.

ITALIAN GARLIC BREAD – BRUSCHETTA

A delicious accompaniment to these wholesome, tasty soups is
Bruschetta, *similar to the French garlic bread, but without all the butter. Ideally it should be grilled over charcoal, so is ideal for trying out at barbecues. Cut thick slices off a crusty loaf. Grill, or toast, and rub with cut cloves of garlic. Trickle over or brush the garlic side with extra virgin olive oil and eat as soon as possible.*

LENTIL AND ANCHOVY SOUP

Ideally, use brown lentils for this soup because they have a better flavour, although red ones are also suitable.

Serves 4–6

1 onion, chopped
1 carrot, chopped
2 sticks celery, chopped
1 clove garlic, crushed
2 tablespoons olive oil
1.75 litres (3 pints) stock or water
2 tablespoons tomato purée
250 g (8 oz) lentils
125 g (4 oz) button mushrooms, sliced
sprig of fresh rosemary
50 g can achovies, drained and chopped
salt and ground black pepper

Sweat the vegetables in the oil in a large covered saucepan over a gentle heat for about 10 minutes. Add the stock, tomato purée, lentils, mushrooms, rosemary and seasoning. (Add salt sparingly at first.) Bring to the boil, then cover and simmer for about an hour, when the lentils should be soft. Red lentils will only take about 40 minutes. Stir in the anchovies, adjust the seasoning and serve hot. However, like most soups, this one improves in flavour if made the day before and re-heated.

When a recipe tells you to 'sweat' vegetables, this means to fry them on the lowest possible heat in a covered saucepan. The steam is contained in the pan and helps to soften the vegetables. It is a particularly healthy way of preparing vegetables, and very popular among chefs!

MUSHROOM AND MARSALA SOUP

Serves 4–8

600 ml (1 pint) milk
1 bay leaf
1 onion, chopped
1 small carrot, sliced
(15 g) ½ oz dried mushrooms (porcini or cèpes)
600 ml (1 pint) boiling water
50 g (2 oz) butter
40 g (1½ oz) flour
375 g (12 oz) fresh mushrooms, open cup or large buttons
1–2 tablespoons Marsala wine
2 tablespoons fresh chopped parsley
salt and ground black pepper

Scald the milk with the bay leaf and a tablespoon of the onion and the carrot, and leave to steep for 15 minutes. Cover the dried mushrooms with the boiling water and leave to steep also for about the same time. Melt the butter and gently fry the remaining onion, without browning, for 5 minutes. Stir in the flour and cook the roux for 1–2 minutes.

Strain the milk, discarding the vegetables, and slowly stir into the roux, mixing until smooth and thickened. Slice a few of the fresh mushrooms, reserve for a garnish, and roughly chop the rest. Add to the pan together with the soaked mushrooms and their liquor. Season, bring to the boil then simmer gently for 20 minutes.

Blend or process the soup until smooth and add the Marsala, parsley and reserved sliced mushrooms. Re-heat gently and simmer for a minute or two, just to cook the mushrooms, then adjust the seasoning. Serve hot.

Note: This soup tastes even better if made the day before up to the simmering stage and then finished the next day.

TUSCAN ROASTED RED PEPPER SOUP

Serves 4–6

1 large red pepper
1 large onion, chopped
1 clove garlic, crushed
2 tablespoons olive oil
2 slices unsmoked bacon, de-rinded and chopped, optional
150 ml (¼ pint) dry red wine, optional
2 x 400 g cans peeled plum tomatoes
1.2 litres (2 pints) stock or water
1 teaspoon dried oregano
1 bay leaf
1 small dried chilli, chopped, optional
a pinch of sugar
salt and ground black pepper

OVEN TEMPERATURE: Gas Mark 7/220°C/425°F

Preheat the oven. Put the pepper, uncut, on a baking sheet and roast for 10–15 minutes until the skin is blackened. Turn once or twice. The skin does not have to be black all over. Cool, then peel off the skin, de-seed and chop, saving any juice. Sauté the onion, garlic and pepper flesh in the oil for 5 minutes until softened. Add the bacon, if using, and fry gently for another 5 minutes, then add the wine, if using, and cook for 2 minutes. Add all the remaining ingredients. Stir well, then simmer, covered, for 30 minutes.

The soup can be left chunky or liquidised or processed until smooth.

> *If you only use part of any canned product, store the rest in a non-metallic container, as there is a danger of tainting if you leave food in the opened can.*

CHICK PEA AND PEPERONI SOUP – Zuppa de ceci

A tasty, colourful main meal soup. The long peperoni sausage can be bought at Italian delicatessens, but if you can't find it, then use French garlic sausage slices, cut in quarters. Also, instead of chick peas, try borlotti beans.

Serves 4

2 leeks, sliced thinly
2 carrots, chopped
2 medium potatoes, chopped
25 g (1 oz) butter
1 tablespoon olive oil
1.5 litres (2½ pints) stock
400 g can chick peas or borlotti beans
3–4 tablespoons long grain rice
50 g (2 oz) sliced peperoni sausage or French garlic sausage slices, cut in quarters
salt and ground black pepper

Sweat the vegetables in the butter and oil in a large covered saucepan for about 10 minutes. Add the stock. Drain the peas' liquor into the pan too. Mash half the chick peas, or beans, with a fork and stir into the pan with the whole peas. Season, bring to the boil and simmer, covered, for about 20 minutes.

Add the rice and sausage, stir well, bring back to the boil and simmer again for about 12 minutes.

LOMBARDY SPICED PUMPKIN SOUP

We tend to associate pumpkins just with Halloween in Britain and use them only for decorative purposes. But not only do they make good pies, the flesh is very tasty turned into soup, especially if lightly spiced.

Serves 4–6

1 onion, chopped
1 clove garlic, crushed
250 g (8 oz) potatoes, peeled and diced
3 tablespoons olive oil
1 small pumpkin, about 1.1 kg (2½ lbs) peeled, de-seeded and diced
1.75 litres (3 pints) stock
1 teaspoon coriander seeds, crushed
large pinch ground cumin
1 bay leaf
150 ml (¼ pint) single cream, optional
salt and ground black pepper
few coriander or flat parsley leaves, to garnish

Sauté the onion, garlic and potatoes in the oil for about 10 minutes, stirring occasionally, without browning. Add the pumpkin flesh, cover and sweat for 5 minutes then pour in the stock, spices, bay and seasoning. Bring to the boil, then simmer, covered, for about 50 minutes until soft.

Strain the vegetables and blend or process until smooth and return to the pan with the stock. Re-heat. Stir in the cream, if liked, and serve hot, garnished with the herb leaves.

CROUTONS – CROSTINI DE PANE

Sprinkle Italian soups with crisply fried bread croutons. Cut ready-sliced, crustless bread into cubes of about 2.5 cm (1 inch). Heat a frying-pan, preferably with a metal chip basket, to 190°C/370°F then fry the bread for about 30 seconds until golden brown. Drain well on a kitchen towel. For convenience, make up a large batch at a time, and store in an air-tight container. When required, simply spread on a baking sheet and re-heat in a low oven to re-crisp.

2 ANTIPASTO

Antipasto means 'served before a meal' – traditionally as an hors d'oeuvre. However, when a number of antipasto dishes are prepared together they make a glorious and colourful buffet – a meal in itself. Because they are so simple to prepare and the ingredients are so varied, even the most inexperienced cook can make a fantastic display.

BAGNA CAUDA

This oil, garlic and anchovy dip originates from Piedmont. It is usually served in a small pot over a burner, with well-chilled vegetables.

Serves 4

150 ml (¼ pint) olive oil
50 g (2 oz) butter
3 large cloves of garlic, crushed
2 × 50 g cans anchovies

VEGETABLES
small bulb fennel
2 sticks celery
2 small carrots
1 red pepper
½ cucumber

Put the oil, butter and garlic into a small saucepan. Drain the anchovy oil in, chop the anchovies and add these as well. Simmer very gently for 5 minutes taking care the garlic does not burn or it will taste bitter. Stir occasionally. Pour into a heatproof container and set on a stand over a spirit burner or candle. Prepare the vegetables into bite-size sticks, and chill well.

Guests take a vegetable stick and dip it into the hot oil, stirring up the sediment each time. The cold vegetables help to cool the oil before it reaches the mouth, but care should still be taken at first!

Bagna Cauda

AFFETTATO –
SLICED MEAT PLATTER

A platter of cold cured meats can look stunning and needs absolutely no cooking – just an artistic eye. Because the meats are sliced thinly, a little goes a long way. Fold or roll some of the meats and arrange them attractively, garnished with slices of lemon, fresh bay leaves, olives, salad leaves, tomatoes, radishes – even evergreen pine leaves. In Italy, small curls of butter are sometimes served with the meat, and crusty white bread or rolls are a must.

Allow 50 g (2 oz) of total meat quantity per head if served with other salads (more if served without), and choose from the following meats, according to availability.

BRESAOLA – very thinly-sliced cured fillet of beef. Trickle over some olive oil and fresh lemon juice just before serving.

MILANESE SALAMI – slightly coarsely grained, often made with pork and beef.

HUNGARIAN SALAMI – a smoked salami, more finely grained than Milano, now produced in Italy.

NEAPOLITAN SALAMI – coarsely-grained pork and beef, flavoured with chilli.

MORTADELLA – finely-ground pork with larger pieces of pork fat. May also contain peppercorns and pistachio nuts. The larger the mortadella, the finer the quality. Not sliced quite as thinly as salami. Sometimes available smoked as Mortadella di Amatrice.

PROSCIUTTO CRUDO – cured hams with a salty/sweet taste, served in wafer thin slices. The best known come from Parma, but others occasionally on sale are San Danielle, Toscano and Veneto.

SPECK – a type of smoked prosciutto originally from Austria but now made in the north of Italy and often included in antipasto.

COPPA – boned, cured and rolled shoulder of pork, sliced very thinly.

CHICORY AND PROSCIUTTO TART

Serves 4

FOR THE PASTRY:

250 g (8 oz) plain flour

125 g (4 oz) margarine or butter

cold water

FOR THE FILLING:

1 small onion, sliced

1 clove garlic, crushed

75 g (3 oz) prosciutto ham or unsmoked lean bacon, de-rinded and sliced

2 tablespoons olive oil

3 medium heads chicory, sliced

125 g (4 oz) Gruyère cheese, grated

2 tablespoons grated parmesan cheese

2 eggs and 1 egg yolk, beaten

300 ml (½ pint) milk

freshly grated nutmeg

salt and ground black pepper

OVEN TEMPERATURES: Gas Mark 6/200°C/400°F   Gas Mark 4/180°C/350°F

Rub together the flour and fat until they resemble fine breadcrumbs, then mix to a firm dough with a little cold water. Wrap in cling film and chill for ½ hour.

Preheat the oven. Sauté the onion, garlic and ham or bacon in the oil for about 5 minutes until softened. Add the chicory and sauté for a further 5 minutes. Reserve.

Roll out and line a 21 cm (8-inch) flan dish with the pastry. Prick the base, line with greaseproof paper and baking beans then bake blind at the higher setting for 20 minutes, removing the paper and beans for the last 5 minutes. Spoon in the onion mixture and sprinkle with the cheeses. Beat the eggs, milk, nutmeg and seasonings together. Pour carefully over the filling. Return to the oven at the lower setting for a further 30 minutes.

Chicory and Prosciutto Tart; Carrot, Fennel and Oregano Salad; Globe Artichokes; Affettato

GLOBE ARTICHOKES

The Italians are very fond of artichokes which are an increasingly regular sight now in Britain. In Italy, they are often sold much younger and more tender, and can be cooked whole and stuffed, or fried. The ones we can buy over here, I feel, are better either eaten as an hors d'oeuvre, with the leaves peeled off and dipped in butter or a sauce, or stripped of their leaves, de-choked and just served as hearts (e.g. in Lamb Fricassee, see page 74).

Serves 4

4 fresh artichokes
½ lemon, cut in slices, plus lemon juice
salt

TO SERVE:
75 g (3 oz) melted butter mixed with a squeeze of fresh lemon juice, or 150 ml (¼ pint) garlic-flavoured mayonnaise

Cut the stalk from the artichokes and trim the leaf tips, to neaten, if you like. Boil in plenty of salted water with the lemon juice for about 45 minutes until a leaf from the base pulls off easily. Turn upside down to drain and cool. When cool enough to handle, part the leaf tops, and pull out the central core of leaves. Retain if possible. Using a sharp teaspoon, scrape out the spiky choke cleaning as much as possible from the exposed heart. Replace the central leaves and reform the artichoke, if necessary.

Serve hot with the butter and lemon juice, or chilled with mayonnaise.

Note: To eat an artichoke, work from the outside in. Pull off the leaves singly and dip the base only in the sauce. Put the fleshy base between your teeth and pull sharply down to scrape off. Discard the leaf. When you reach the heart, eat it with a knife and fork, dipping in the sauce.

CARROT, FENNEL AND OREGANO SALAD

Serves 4–6

500 g (1 lb) carrots, peeled thinly
1 small bulb fennel
juice of 1 lemon
3 tablespoons extra virgin olive oil
2 tablespoons fresh chopped oregano, or 1 teaspoon dried and 2 tablespoons fresh oregano
chopped parsley
salt and ground black pepper
rings of red onion, to garnish

Coarsely grate the carrots and fennel into a large bowl using a grater or processor. Toss in the lemon juice, oil, herbs and seasoning. Cover and chill for an hour or two before serving. Garnish with the onion.

Oil is graded according to how soon after picking the olives are pressed, and at which stage of the pressing the oil is collected. No heat or chemicals are involved, so the 'juice' is quite pure and natural. The first pressing produces the top grade – extra virgin, (a Napolina product) with a maximum acidity of only 1 per cent. Then follows superfine virgin oil with 1.5 per cent; fine virgin oil at 3 per cent; pure olive oil (also a Napolina product) at 3.5 per cent, which contains a blend of refined and virgin oil, and the last category which is simply called olive oil.

Like wine and cheeses, olive oils have different characteristics of aroma and colour depending on where they are grown. A good general rule when deciding which oil to use is: the simpler the recipe, the better the oil should be.

3 PASTA DISHES AND SAUCES

PESTO SAUCE

Fresh basil leaves and good olive oil are essential for this sauce. You'll need quite a lot of basil leaves. Although traditionally made with pine kernels, Pesto is equally delicious made with walnuts. It is generally tossed into freshly cooked pasta, but is also good with boiled potatoes, or stirred into soups. This is sufficient for about 250 g (8 oz) dried pasta.

Serves 4

fresh basil leaves to fill a 300 ml (½ pint) mug
50 g (2 oz) pine kernels or chopped walnuts
2 cloves of garlic, crushed
good pinch of rock salt
80 g drum of parmesan cheese
8 tablespoons extra virgin olive oil or 5 tablespoons olive oil and 40 g (1½ oz) softened butter

If you have a pestle and mortar, grind the basil and nuts together to a smooth paste with the garlic and salt. Gradually work in the cheese, oil and butter, if using. If using a food processor or liquidiser then blend everything together. Just before serving, mix in about 2 tablespoons of the pasta cooking water to thin the sauce a little, and make it easier to toss.

Note: You can make up larger quantities of this sauce which will store well in the fridge, especially if covered with a thin layer of olive oil.

Pesto Sauce

HOME-MADE TOMATO SAUCE – Salsa pomodoro

You need never be at a loss for a good meal with a couple of cans of tomatoes, olive oil, an onion, and a pack of pasta in your cupboard. A good tomato sauce is one of the easiest recipes to make, and it takes next to no time to cook. This is enough for 375 g (12 oz) dried pasta.

Serves 4

1 large onion, chopped
1–2 cloves garlic, crushed
3 tablespoons olive oil, preferably extra virgin
2 × 400 g cans peeled plum or chopped tomatoes
1 tablespoon fresh chopped marjoram, or basil, or oregano, or 1 teaspoon dried mixed herbs
½ teaspoon sugar
salt and ground black pepper
grated parmesan cheese, to sprinkle

Sauté the onion and garlic in the oil for about 5 minutes until softened. Add the tomatoes, mashing slightly with a fork if whole plum tomatoes. Bring to the boil. Add the herbs, sugar and seasoning. Simmer uncovered for about 20 minutes, stirring occasionally. Toss into freshly cooked pasta just before serving, and sprinkle with grated parmesan.

VARIATIONS

○ Add a finely chopped carrot and stick of celery with the onion and garlic
○ Add 50 g (2 oz) unsmoked bacon, diced, with the onion and garlic
○ Add 125 g (4 oz) button mushrooms, sliced, with the herbs, sugar and seasoning
○ For a special sauce – add all three variations!

BÉCHAMEL SAUCE –
Salsa besciamella

Serves 4

600 ml (1 pint) milk
1 small onion
1 large bay leaf
1 medium carrot, quartered
50 g (2 oz) butter
40 g (1½ oz) flour
salt and ground black pepper
freshly grated nutmeg, optional

Scald the milk to almost boiling with the onion, bay leaf and carrot. Remove from the heat and allow to stand for at least 15 minutes, preferably longer. Melt the butter in a saucepan and stir in the flour to form a smooth roux. Allow to cook gently, without over-browning, for about a minute. Strain the milk and gradually pour into the roux, stirring with a wooden spoon or, better still, a whisk. To avoid getting any lumps, only add more milk when the previous amount has been smoothly incorporated. Season with salt, pepper and nutmeg, if liked. Allow to simmer very gently for about 10 minutes, stirring occasionally to prevent the bottom burning. Use as required.

SALAMI AND RED PEPPER SAUCE

Serves 4

1 large onion, sliced thinly

1 red pepper, de-seeded and sliced

1 clove garlic, crushed

2–3 tablespoons olive oil

2 × 400 g cans chopped tomatoes with chillies

1 teaspoon dried oregano or marjoram

50 g (2 oz) mortadella sausage, chopped

50 g (2 oz) salami sausage, chopped

salt and ground black pepper

parmesan cheese, to sprinkle

Sauté the onion, pepper and garlic in the oil for 5 minutes until softened. Add the tomatoes with chillies, herbs and seasoning. Bring to the boil and simmer for about 10 minutes. Add the sausages, and simmer for about 2 minutes. Toss the sauce into the freshly cooked pasta and serve immediately with parmesan cheese.

PROSCIUTTO AND CREAM SAUCE

Serves 3–4

25 g (1 oz) butter

1 clove garlic, crushed

75 g (3 oz) prosciutto ham, or very thinly sliced unsmoked back bacon

175 ml (6 fl oz) single cream

2–3 tablespoons fresh chopped parsley

salt, ground black pepper and freshly grated nutmeg

parmesan cheese, to sprinkle

Melt the butter and gently sauté the garlic and ham or bacon for about 2 minutes. Stir in the other ingredients, and re-heat until nearly boiling. Toss immediately into freshly cooked pasta, and sprinkle well with parmesan cheese.

BOLOGNESE SAUCE –
Ragu Bolognese

The basis of many classic pasta dishes, and so it's well worth making in double or triple quantity, freezing the extra for another time. It is best made the day before, to allow the flavours to mature and develop.

Serves 4

500 g (1 lb) lean minced beef

75 g (3 oz) unsmoked, de-rinded bacon, diced

125 g (4 oz) chicken livers, chopped finely

2–4 tablespoons olive oil

1 large onion, chopped

1 medium carrot, chopped

2 sticks celery, chopped

2 cloves garlic, crushed

150 ml (¼ pint) dry white or red wine

2 × 400 g cans peeled plum tomatoes or chopped tomatoes

3 tablespoons tomato purée

3 tablespoons single cream, optional

salt and ground black pepper

Using a large saucepan and on a high heat, brown the mince, bacon and livers in 2 tablespoons of the oil. Remove with a slotted spoon and put to one side. Add extra oil to the pan if necessary, then sauté the onion, carrot, celery and garlic for about 5 minutes until softened. Return the meat. Add the wine, and cook until evaporated, then stir in the tomatoes, purée and seasoning. Bring to the boil, then cover and simmer gently for about an hour, stirring occasionally. Uncover for the last 20 minutes to allow some of the liquid to evaporate. Check the seasoning. If liked, stir in the cream before serving or re-heating.

WHOLE MUSHROOM AND GORGONZOLA SAUCE

Serves 4

250 g (8 oz) button mushrooms
2 tablespoons olive oil
1 clove garlic, crushed, optional
300 ml (½ pint) single cream
175 g (6 oz) Gorgonzola cheese, de-rinded and crumbled
salt and ground black pepper
2 tablespoons fresh chopped parsley, to serve

Sauté the mushrooms gently in the oil with the garlic, if using, in a covered saucepan for 5 minutes, shaking the pan occasionally. Add the cream and bring to the boil. Simmer for 2 minutes. Stir in the cheese and re-heat, but do not allow to boil. Add pepper, but taste before adding salt, as the cheese can be enough. Toss immediately into cooked pasta and serve sprinkled with parsley.

Add a couple of tablespoonfuls of oil to the water when boiling pasta – it helps to stop it from boiling over, and prevents it from sticking together. Don't overdrain pasta after cooking – leave it slightly wet, as they do in Italy. Or re-moisten it with a little hot stock, then toss in some extra virgin olive oil, salt, ground black pepper, and a little freshly grated nutmeg.

PIEDMONT VEAL AND MUSHROOM SAUCE

Serves 4

15 g (½ oz) dried porcini mushrooms
300 ml (½ pint) hot water
1 onion, chopped
2 cloves garlic, crushed
2 carrots, chopped
2 sticks celery, chopped
2 rashers unsmoked bacon, de-rinded and chopped
25 g (1 oz) butter
2 tablespoons olive oil
250 g (8 oz) minced veal (or pork)
150 ml (¼ pint) dry white wine
400 g can chopped tomatoes
250 g (8 oz) button mushrooms, sliced
½ stock cube
1 bay leaf
1 sprig thyme or ½ teaspoon dried thyme
4 cloves or a good pinch of ground cloves
salt and ground black pepper
grated parmesan cheese, to serve

Cover the porcini with 300 ml (½ pint) hot water and leave for about 15 minutes. Drain, reserving the liquor, and chop. Sauté the onion, garlic, carrots, celery and bacon in the butter and oil for 5 minutes. Add the veal (or pork) and fry for another 5 minutes. Pour in the wine, then stir in the tomatoes and mushrooms. Sprinkle in the stock cube, herbs and cloves, and simmer for about 25 minutes. Adjust the seasoning. Remove the bay leaf and cloves, if using whole ones. Serve hot, tossed into freshly cooked pasta and sprinkled with grated parmesan cheese.

HOME-MADE FRESH PASTA

There are times, such as when you wish to make your own ravioli or other filled pasta shapes, when it is very rewarding to make your own pasta – if only to appreciate good quality ready-made dried pasta on other occasions!

The process is quite simple, but it does take time, even if you have a special pasta-rolling machine. You will need, in addition to a lot of work space, 2 or 3 clean tea towels on which to spread out the pasta to dry.

Use a good strong (bread) flour, allowing 1 egg for each 100 g (3½ oz), plus a little olive oil to keep the dough supple. Initial mixing and kneading can be done in a mixer or food processor. After mixing, the dough is rolled several times until it is smooth and elastic, after which it is cut into shapes or noodles. Cooking takes next to no time, just a few minutes.

Serves 3–4

300 g (10 oz) strong plain flour, sifted with 1 teaspoon salt
3 eggs, beaten
1 tablespoon olive oil

Mix the flour, salt, eggs and oil together until they form a firm but soft dough. Divide the dough into three pieces, if rolling out by hand, or into 6 small balls, if using a pasta-rolling machine. To roll by hand: on a lightly floured board, using a rolling pin, roll out to the thickness of a 10p piece, then fold into three, and re-roll slightly thinner. Repeat this process about 5 or 6 times, making the dough thinner each time, then use as required. Keep the remainder of the dough covered whilst rolling the rest.

To roll by machine, follow the instructions, feeding the small balls of dough through the rollers and adjusting the thickness as required.

Lay the dough sheets out on clean tea towels to dry. Even if needed in sheets, fresh pasta dough is easier to handle if slightly dry.

Note: To cut into noodles, roll each sheet up into a 'sausage' and cut horizontally across, unravelling into strips. Place back on the towels, swirled into nest shapes, to dry a bit.

To cut into ravioli, use small pastry cutters, about 4 cm (1½ inches) in diameter, or simply use a rotating pasta-cutting wheel.

LASAGNE AL FORNO

So many dreadful ready-prepared dishes are sold by the name of Lasagne, that a good home-made one can come as a very pleasant surprise. For a start, the pasta must have a good bite to it, and sheets of Napolina oven-ready Lasagnetta are ideal. It is not difficult to make your own lasagne, but there are a number of stages. I like to make mine the day before, because it helps 'set' the sauces, and makes cooking and serving much easier.

Serves 4–6

1 recipe quantity of Ragu Bolognese (see page 29)
1½ times recipe quantity of Béchamel sauce (see page 27)
8 sheets Napolina Oven-ready Lasagnetta
80 g drum parmesan cheese, plus extra to serve

OVEN TEMPERATURE: Gas Mark 5/190°C/375°F

Grease a medium sized au gratin or casserole dish. Spread about a quarter of the Ragu on the base. Arrange sheets of Napolina oven-ready lasagnetta on top, breaking to fit, if necessary, and making sure they do not overlap too much. Spoon over enough Béchamel to cover the pasta, sprinkle well with parmesan, then layer with Ragu. Repeat the layers, ending with Ragu and Béchamel which you can swirl attractively together. Sprinkle with the rest of the parmesan. Ideally, chill for a few hours or overnight before baking. To cook, bake for about ½ hour until bubbling and cooked. Allow to stand for 10 minutes or so for easier cutting.

Hand round extra parmesan, if liked, for serving. All you need is a crisp green salad to accompany this, and maybe slices of *Bruschetta*, Italian garlic bread (see page 10).

Note: For special occasions, add about 250 g (8 oz) of sliced peperoni sausage to the Ragu, and include layers of Italian curd ricotta cheese.

Such a special dish deserves a good wine. Choose any D.O.C. quality dry red wine, especially those with a Classico or Superiore classification like a Chianti (look for a black cockerel on the cork label) or Valpolicella.

PASTA SHELLS WITH ARTICHOKES, LEEKS AND BACON

We are becoming more familiar with artichokes in this country now, but tend to eat them only as a starter. In Italy, they eat them smaller and younger, before the chokes become inedible. Use either fresh artichoke hearts for this recipe, or canned artichoke hearts in brine.

Serves 4

3 fresh artichokes or a 375 g can artichoke hearts in brine, drained
a squeeze of lemon juice
200 g (7 oz) pasta shells
2 leeks, sliced in rings
3 rashers unsmoked bacon, de-rinded and sliced
1 clove garlic, crushed
3 tablespoons olive oil
150 ml (¼ pint) dry white wine, optional
125 g (4 oz) frozen peas
300 ml (½ pint) single cream
3 tablespoons grated parmesan cheese
salt and ground black pepper

If using fresh artichokes, pull off the leaves and discard. Cut off the spiky choke, leaving only the hearts. Drop these into some cold water, with a squeeze of lemon juice to prevent oxidation, whilst you prepare the other artichokes. Boil all three in slightly salted water for 15 minutes until just tender, then slice and reserve. If using canned artichokes, cut each heart into quarters. Boil the pasta shells according to pack instructions. Drain, rinse and keep warm. Sauté the leeks, bacon and garlic in the oil for 5 minutes. Add the wine, if using, let it bubble down for 2 minutes, then stir in the artichoke hearts, peas and seasoning. Cook for 5 minutes. Stir in the cream, re-heat until almost boiling, and toss into the pasta. Serve immediately, sprinkled with the cheese.

PASTA SHAPES WITH CHICKEN AND SAFFRON SAUCE

Serves 4

a good pinch of saffron strands
300 ml (½ pint) hot light stock
250 g (8 oz) pasta shapes
25 g (1 oz) butter
250 g (8 oz) skinned chicken breast, sliced thinly into strips
1 tablespoon olive oil
150 ml (¼ pint) single cream
2 egg yolks, beaten
2 tablespoons fresh chopped parsley
salt and ground black pepper
parmesan cheese, to sprinkle

Soak the saffron in the stock for about 10 minutes. Meanwhile, boil the pasta according to pack instructions. Drain then toss in half the butter and keep warm. Sauté the chicken strips in the remaining butter and oil, stirring occasionally, for about 2 minutes to brown lightly. Pour the saffron-flavoured stock in with the strips, and bubble up for about 5 minutes, stirring occasionally. Season. Pour in the cream, bring back to the boil and simmer for a minute. Remove from the heat and stir in the egg yolks. The sauce should thicken slightly without further cooking. Toss into the pasta together with the parsley and serve as soon as possible with parmesan cheese, if liked.

Tagliatelle with Chicken and Saffron Sauce; Rigatoni with Tuna and Black Olives;
Tagliatelle with Smoked Salmon and Broccoli

RIGATONI WITH TUNA AND BLACK OLIVES

Serves 4

250 g (8 oz) dried rigatoni pasta
1 tablespoon butter
1 onion, sliced thinly
1 clove garlic, crushed
2 tablespoons olive oil, preferably extra virgin
2 × 400 g cans peeled plum tomatoes or chopped tomatoes
2 medium courgettes, sliced
1 teaspoon dried oregano or marjoram
170 g can tuna in oil, drained and flaked
75 g (3 oz) pitted black olives, halved
2–3 tablespoons fresh chopped parsley
salt and ground black pepper

Cook the rigatoni according to pack instructions. Drain, toss in the butter and keep warm. Meanwhile, sauté the onion and garlic in the oil for 5 minutes, then add the tomatoes, mashing with a fork, if plum tomatoes. Add the courgettes, herbs and seasoning. Bring to the boil, simmer for 10 minutes, then stir in the tuna and olives. Repeat, and add the parsley. Adjust the seasoning and toss into the pasta.

PASTA QUILLS WITH TOMATOES AND CHICK PEAS

Serves 4

250 g (8 oz) pasta quills
3 tablespoons olive oil, preferably extra virgin
1 onion, chopped
1 clove garlic, crushed
3 rashers unsmoked streaky bacon de-rinded and chopped, optional
400 g can chopped tomatoes with herbs
2 tablespoons tomato purée

400 g can chick peas

salt and ground black pepper

parmesan cheese, to sprinkle

Cook the pasta according to pack instructions. Drain and toss in 1 tablespoon of oil. Keep warm. Sauté the onion, garlic and bacon in the remaining oil for 5 minutes. Add the tomatoes with herbs, purée, and seasoning and simmer for a further 5 minutes. Season and stir in the chick peas and their liquor. Re-heat, then toss in the pasta. Serve immediately.

TAGLIATELLE WITH SMOKED SALMON AND BROCCOLI

Serves 4–6

250 g (8 oz) tagliatelle, green or white

25 g (1 oz) butter

375 g (12 oz) broccoli florets, trimmed of thick stalks

300 ml (½ pint) single cream

125–175 g (4–6 oz) smoked salmon (off-cuts would be fine), cut in strips

1 tablespoon fresh chopped dill or fennel

salt and ground black pepper

sprigs of dill or fennel, to garnish

Cook the tagliatelle according to pack instructions. Drain and rinse, then toss in the butter. Put into a warm shallow serving dish and keep warm. Meanwhile, boil the broccoli until just cooked – *'al dente'* – for about 3 minutes, in the minimum of lightly salted water. Drain and return to the pan. Pour over the cream and re-heat. Carefully stir in the salmon and herbs, re-heat and season. Pour over the tagliatelle and serve immediately.

When a recipe or cooking instruction tells you to cook pasta or vegetables until 'al dente' – 'to the tooth', it means until it is only just cooked and still has some bite, not soft and overcooked. For pasta, cooking times vary according to the thickness and shape of it, so follow pack instructions for complete success.

HOME-MADE SPINACH RAVIOLI

Makes about 60 to serve 4–6

FOR THE PASTA:

200 g (7 oz) strong plain flour

½ teaspoon salt

2 eggs, beaten

1 tablespoon olive oil

125 g (4 oz) spinach, cooked, squeezed dry and chopped

FOR THE FILLING:

1 small onion, chopped

2 tablespoons olive oil

125 g (4 oz) fresh mushrooms, finely chopped

50 g (2 oz) walnuts, finely chopped or 125 g (4 oz) cooked ham, minced

125 g (4 oz) ricotta cheese

2 tablespoons grated parmesan cheese

1 tablespoon fresh marjoram, chopped

salt and ground black pepper

Make up the pasta (see page 32), adding in the spinach with the eggs. Mix the filling ingredients together. Roll out the pasta and cut into 5 cm (2–inch) rounds, using a pastry-cutter. Do this in batches. Put small amounts of filling on one side of each round, fold over and press to seal. If you like, bring the corners round and press together to form little hat shapes, or 'capelletti'. Lay out on clean tea towels to dry. Boil for just 5 minutes in lightly salted water until *'al dente'*, and toss in a little butter with parmesan cheese. Ravioli is also good served with the tomato sauce on page 26.

Note: Home-made ravioli freezes very well, or if sufficiently dried, can be stored in the fridge, interleaved with kitchen towel, until required.

Home-made Spinach Ravioli; Pork and Pasta Mould

PORK AND PASTA MOULD

Serves 4–6

200 g (7 oz) pasta bows, shells, elbows or macaroni

600 ml (1 pint) milk

1 bay leaf

1 small onion, sliced

1 small carrot, sliced

50 g (2 oz) butter

3 tablespoons natural dried breadcrumbs

40 g (1½ oz) flour

4 tablespoons grated parmesan cheese

freshly grated nutmeg

FOR THE MEAT LAYER:

75 g (3 oz) unsmoked bacon, chopped

250 g (8 oz) minced pork

1 clove garlic

1 tablespoon olive oil

3 tablespoons freshly chopped parsley

salt and ground black pepper

OVEN TEMPERATURE: Gas Mark 4/180°C/350°F

Preheat the oven. Cook the pasta according to pack instructions. Drain and rinse. Bring the milk slowly to the boil with the bay leaf, onion and carrot. Allow to stand for 15 minutes, then strain. Melt 15 g (½ oz) of the butter, and brush the inside of a 900 ml (1½-pint) pudding basin with it. Coat evenly with the breadcrumbs. Make a roux by melting the remaining butter, stirring in the flour, and cooking for 1 minute. Add the strained milk gradually. Stir in the cheese, and season, adding nutmeg to taste. Simmer for a minute then mix with the pasta.

Fry the bacon, pork and garlic in the oil, stirring occasionally until lightly browned – about 10 minutes. Season and add the parsley.

Layer the pasta and meat, ending with the pasta. Cover with some lightly greased foil, then bake for about 25 minutes. Allow to stand for a few minutes, before turning the mould out onto a hot plate. Serve as soon as possible, accompanied by tomato sauce.

LENTIL AND RICOTTA CANNELLONI

Serves 4–6

8 sheets Napolina oven-ready Lasagnetta
1 onion, chopped
2 sticks celery, chopped
1 small green pepper, de-seeded and chopped
2 cloves garlic, crushed
2 tablespoons olive oil
600 ml (1 pint) stock or water
250 g (8 oz) red lentils
125 g (4 oz) fresh mushrooms, sliced
1 large bay leaf
1 teaspoon dried oregano or marjoram
175 g (6 oz) ricotta cheese
50 g (2 oz) butter, melted
½ × 80 g drum grated parmesan cheese
salt and ground black pepper
Tomato sauce (from page 26)

OVEN TEMPERATURE: Gas Mark 4/180°C/350°F

Preheat the oven. Boil the Lasagnetta sheets for just a minute, to soften. Drain, rinse and lay out on kitchen towels until required. Sweat the vegetables and garlic in the oil in a covered saucepan for 10 minutes. Add the stock, lentils, mushrooms, herbs and seasonings. Bring to the boil, then simmer, covered, for about 25 minutes, stirring occasionally, until thick. Spread ricotta cheese on each of the Lasagnetta sheets, then divide the lentil filling on top. Roll up, not too tightly, and place, join side down, in a shallow ovenproof casserole that has been lightly greased with half the butter. Brush the remaining butter on top of the rolls and sprinkle well with the parmesan cheese. Cover with foil and cook in the oven for about 20 minutes; then uncover to brown lightly for about 10–15 minutes. Serve hot with tomato sauce poured over each serving.

SPAGHETTI CARBONARA

Pasta cooked in the style of the 'carbonara' – the charcoal burners. The secret is to time the cooking of the spaghetti to coincide with the bacon, so that all can be tossed together, and the heat of the spaghetti will be sufficient just to set the eggs, to make a lovely creamy sauce.

Serves 4

375 g (12 oz) spaghetti, plain or wholemeal

2 tablespoons olive oil, preferably extra virgin

3–4 eggs, beaten

2 tablespoons single cream, optional

1 clove garlic, crushed, optional

75–175 g (3–6 oz) smoked streaky bacon, de-rinded and chopped

salt and ground black pepper

grated parmesan cheese, to serve

Boil the spaghetti according to pack instructions. Drain. Toss in one tablespoon of the oil. Meanwhile, beat the eggs with the seasoning, and cream, if using. Sauté the garlic (if using) and bacon in the remaining tablespoon of oil until nearly crisp. Toss the eggs and bacon immediately into the hot spaghetti. Stir quickly and spoon onto warm serving plates. Sprinkle with lots of parmesan cheese.

SPINACH CANNELLONI

An excellent and very pretty first course.

Blanch, squeeze dry and chop 500 g (1 lb) fresh spinach. Mix with 250 g (8 oz) ricotta, curd or cottage cheese, 3 tablespoons grated parmesan cheese, salt, ground black pepper and nutmeg to season. Fill, roll and cook as the Lentil cannelloni recipe (see page 43) (dressing with the melted butter and extra cheese as in the recipe) and serve with the tomato sauce on page 26.

SPAGHETTI WITH SICILIAN SOUR AND SWEET VEGETABLES

Serves 4

1 medium aubergine, cut in sticks
2 medium courgettes, cut in sticks
1 onion, sliced thinly
1 clove garlic, crushed
1 large red pepper, de-seeded and sliced
3 tablespoons olive oil
500 g carton creamed tomatoes
2 tablespoons wine vinegar
juice of 1 lemon
1 tablespoon sugar
2 tablespoons capers
300 ml (½ pint) water
500 g (1 lb) spaghetti
50 g can anchovies, drained and chopped, optional
salt and ground black pepper

Put the aubergine and courgette sticks in a colander and sprinkle lightly, but evenly, with salt. Leave to drain for half an hour, then rinse well in cold running water. Sauté the onion, garlic and pepper in 2 tablespoons of oil for 5 minutes until just softened. Add the tomatoes, vinegar, lemon, sugar and capers. Bring to the boil, add the aubergine and courgettes and 300 ml (½ pint) water. Season (lightly with salt), cover, and simmer for 10 minutes, stirring occasionally. Meanwhile, boil the spaghetti according to pack instructions. Drain, and toss in the remaining tablespoon of oil. If using, add the anchovies to the vegetables, stirring well, and check the seasoning. Serve the sauce either tossed into the spaghetti or alongside it.

4 PIZZA, RICE AND GNOCCHI DISHES

POTATO GNOCCHI –

For best results use floury potatoes like Desirée or Maris Piper (King Edwards, though, do not make good gnocchi.) A beaten egg can be added for richer gnocchi, but eggless ones are supposed to be lighter.

Serves 4–6

750 g (1½ lb) potatoes, peeled weight
175–250 g (6–8 oz) plain flour
1 egg, beaten, optional
salt and ground black pepper
melted butter, to serve

Cut the potatoes into even-sized pieces so they are cooked at the same time without breaking up. Boil in lightly salted water until just cooked, about 12 minutes. Drain and return to the pan over the heat to dry out a little. Mash thoroughly so there are no lumps. Beat in the flour until you have a firm dough. The amount depends on how floury the potatoes are. If you like, a little beaten egg can be added, but don't make the mixture too soft. Season well. On a well floured board, divide and roll the mixture into four long 'sausages'. Make the gnocchi in batches. Put a pan of water onto a rolling boil. Cut each sausage into 12 rounds, and with your hands shape into little discs, pressing a recess in the centre. This makes for even cooking. Drop each batch into the boiling water and when the gnocchi rises to the top, after about 30 seconds, scoop out with a slotted spoon and into a warm serving dish. Drizzle with a little melted butter. Repeat with the remaining batches. Serve with grated parmesan or a Napolina sauce.

Note: In Italy, the gnocchi rounds are pressed into the prongs of a fork to form a pattern.

CALZONE

This is something of a cross between a filled pitta bread and hot, freshly baked pizza. It is great fun to bake Calzones for an al fresco party, handing them around on a tray with glasses of crisp, chilled Italian white wine.

Serves 4–8

500 g (1 lb) strong plain bread flour
1 tablespoon salt
1 sachet fast action yeast
about 300 ml (½ pint) warm water
150 g (5 oz) pack mozzarella cheese, sliced into 8
8 slices of prosciutto ham or 16 slices Italian salami
grated parmesan cheese, to sprinkle
dried oregano, to sprinkle
olive oil, to brush
salt and ground black pepper

OVEN TEMPERATURE: Gas Mark 6/200°C/400°F

Mix the flour and salt, then blend in the yeast. Mix to a firm dough with the water, adding more or less as required. Knead the dough well, either by hand on a lightly floured board or in a food processor, until smooth and elastic. Cover with oiled cling film and leave to prove in a warm place until doubled in size. Preheat the oven. Knock the dough out and knead again. Divide into 8 balls. Roll each dough piece out to an oblong about 15 × 10 cm (6 × 4 inches). Brush the edges with a little water. Put a slice of mozzarella cheese and prosciutto ham, or 2 slices each of salami, on one half of each dough piece. Sprinkle with parmesan, oregano and seasoning. Fold in half and press well to seal. Brush the tops with oil and place on lightly oiled baking sheets. Bake for about 20 minutes until risen, crisp and golden. This can be done in 2 batches without the dough suffering, as it can be stored in the fridge whilst waiting to be cooked. Serve as soon as possible.

HOME-MADE PIZZAS

Serves 4

1 large onion, sliced

2 cloves garlic, crushed

2 tablespoons olive oil

2 × 400 g cans chopped tomatoes with herbs

425 g (14 oz) mozzarella cheese, sliced thinly

salt and ground black pepper

FOR THE BASE:

500 g (1 lb) strong flour, white or wholemeal or a mixture of both

1 teaspoon salt

1 sachet fast action or easy blend yeast

1 tablespoon olive oil

about 200 ml (7 fl oz) warm water

TOPPING IDEAS:

Choose from a selection of: strips of ham, sliced salami or peperoni, snipped anchovies, flaked tuna, sliced cooked mushrooms, blanched and well-drained spinach, olives, grated parmesan cheese.

OVEN TEMPERATURE: Gas Mark 6/200°C/400°F

Preheat the oven. Sauté the onion and garlic in the oil for about 5 minutes until softened. Add the tomatoes with herbs, and seasonings. Simmer for 15 minutes, stirring occasionally, until thickened. Cool.

Now start on the base. Mix the flour, salt and yeast together. Blend in the oil and water. (*Note:* do not mix fast-action yeast with water first, or it will not work.) Knead well together until smooth and elastic. If the mixture seems a little dry then add extra water. Divide into four. On a lightly floured board, roll or pat out each dough piece to a round about 20 cm (8 inches) wide. (Alternatively, you can make eight mini-pizzas, half this size.) Place on flat, greased, baking sheets. Spread the filling on the pizza bases. Top with the mozzarella, then your chosen toppings. Allow to prove for 15 minutes. Bake for 12–15 minutes.

Home-made Pizzas

MOZZARELLA IN CARROZZA

This is really like our eggy bread and cheese on toast combined – it's delicious. The name means 'in a carriage', and the cheese is sandwiched between slices of bread. If you can't find mozzarella, then use bel paese cheese instead.

Serves 4

150 g (5 oz) piece mozzarella, cut in 12 thin slices

8 slices thin sandwich bread, crusts removed

3 eggs (size 1 or 2), beaten

olive oil for frying

salt

Put 3 slices of cheese each onto 4 slices of bread. Top with the other 4 bread slices and press firmly together. Put the eggs, seasoned, into a shallow dish or roasting pan. Press both sides of the sandwiches in well. Leave to soak for 20 minutes, turning carefully once, to make sure all the egg is absorbed.

Pour about 5 mm (¼ inch) of oil into a thick-based frying pan and heat well. Fry the sandwiches on both sides until golden brown and crisp. Drain on kitchen towel and serve as soon as possible.

DEEP-FRIED MOZZARELLA

Mozzarella is also delicious coated, crumbed and deep-fried. Cut into slices, dip in flour and beaten egg, then dried breadcrumbs mixed with a pinch of dried oregano and some grated parmesan cheese. Deep fry for 1–2 minutes in hot oil. Drain and serve quickly.

SPINACH SEMOLINA GNOCCHI

Serves 4–6

750 ml (1¼ pints) milk
200 g (7 oz) coarse semolina
50 g (2 oz) butter, half of it melted
80 g drum grated parmesan cheese
freshly grated nutmeg
2 eggs, beaten
125 g (4 oz) frozen leaf spinach, thawed, squeezed dry and chopped
salt and ground black pepper

TO SERVE:
Extra grated parmesan cheese, Tomato sauce from page 26, or 411 g can
Napolina Tomato and bacon or Tomato and mushroom sauce

OVEN TEMPERATURE: Gas Mark 5/190°C/375°F

Preheat the oven. Put the milk on to boil in a large saucepan. When just on
the point of boiling, slowly sprinkle in the semolina, stirring until smooth.
Cook, still stirring, until very thick, then simmer on a low heat for about 2
minutes. Remove from the heat and mix in the solid half of butter, cheese,
nutmeg to taste and seasoning. Cool slightly, then beat in the eggs. If you
like plain gnocchi as well, divide the mixture into two. Leave one half plain,
but beat in the chopped spinach (which should be quite dry) into the other
half. Spoon the mixture/s onto large flat boards or plates, to a 1 cm
(½ inch) thickness. Smooth the tops, cool, then chill until solid. Using plain
scone cutters or upturned glasses of about 4 cm (1½ inches) in diameter,
cut out as many rounds as possible. Leftover mixture can be moulded
together and shaped roughly for the underneath. Lightly grease a shallow
ovenproof dish and arrange the gnocchi circles in it, overlapping. If you've
made plain ones, then alternate these with the spinach ones. Put
misshapen circles underneath. Brush the tops with the remaining butter
and sprinkle over more cheese, about 2–3 tablespoons. Bake for about
30–40 minutes until golden and crisp on top. Serve as soon as possible with
hot sauce.

Seafood Risotto; Mozzarella in Carrozza; Spinach Semolina Gnocchi

RISOTTO MILANESE

Italian risottos should be served moist and creamy, not dry and fluffy like pilaffs. The best quality risotto rice is arborio, available from specialist delicatessens, but other suitable kinds are now more easily available from many supermarkets.

For the classic Milanese risotto you need good home-made chicken broth (see page 6), and if your butcher has any, marrow from veal shin bones (the same cut for Ossobuco, see page 75). This dish is very tasty on its own, or as the classic accompaniment to Ossobuco, or can have chopped ham, chicken and peas added for a more substantial dish.

Serves 4

1 tablespoon extra virgin olive oil
40 g (1½ oz) butter
1 small onion or shallot, chopped
1 clove garlic, crushed
about 2 tablespoons raw veal marrow, chopped, optional
pinch of saffron strands
2 tablespoons hot water
250 g (8 oz) arborio risotto rice
150 m (¼ pint) dry white wine
900 ml (1½ pints) chicken broth or stock
½ × 80 g drum parmesan cheese
salt and ground black pepper

> *Peel onions tearlessly under cold running water, and do not remove the root end until after chopping. Also, Spanish onions are gentler than English or Egyptian, so use those if your eyes are prone to weeping!*

Heat the oil and a third of the butter in a thick-based saucepan. Gently sauté, without browning, the onion, garlic and marrow, if using, for 5 minutes. Soak the saffron strands in 2 tablespoons hot water. Add the rice to the pan and fry, stirring occasionally for a couple of minutes until opaque. Pour in the wine and cook until absorbed, approximately 3 minutes. Pour in a third of the broth or stock, bring to the boil, season and stir well. Simmer gently, uncovered, until the broth or stock has been nearly absorbed. Add a little more liquid, stir and cook again gently. Continue like this, adding the broth or stock gradually until the rice is cooked. This technique is essential for the right creamy texture and should take about 20 minutes in all. Add the saffron strands and soaking water. Stir in the remaining butter and parmesan cheese. Serve as soon as possible.

SEAFOOD RISOTTO

Serves 3–4

FOR THE BASE:

2 tablespoons extra virgin olive oil

1 small onion or shallot, chopped

250 g (8 oz) risotto rice

150 ml (¼ pint) dry white wine

900 ml (1½ pints) hot fish stock or water

½ × 80 g drum grated parmesan cheese

FOR THE SEAFOOD INGREDIENTS:

25 g (1 oz) butter

1 clove garlic, crushed

about 16 mussels, in shells, scrubbed

250 g (8 oz) prawns in shells or 125 g (4 oz) shelled prawns

125 g (4 oz) button mushrooms, sliced

2 tablespoons cognac, optional

3 tablespoons fresh chopped parsley

salt and ground black pepper

Make the risotto base as for Risotto Milanese (see page opposite), but without the saffron, and substituting fish stock or water for the chicken broth. Towards the end of cooking, in a separate pan melt the butter and gently sauté the garlic. Add the mussels, cover and cook for about 5 minutes until the mussels open. Discard any that haven't. Add the prawns and cook them, uncovered, for about 3 minutes. Add the mushrooms, then the cognac, if using, and reduce down. Stir in the parsley then mix in the risotto. Check the seasoning and serve as soon as possible.

RISI E BISI

A cross between a risotto and soup, this famous, delicious and simple Venetian dish is served at banquets to celebrate St Mark's Day. Ideal for a light meal.

Serves 4

1 small onion, chopped
2 rashers unsmoked bacon, de-rinded and chopped
50 g (2 oz) butter
175 g (6 oz) risotto rice
1.2 litre (2 pints) chicken or vegetable stock
½ stock cube
½ teaspoon sugar
375 g (12 oz) young peas, fresh or frozen
½ × 80 g drum grated parmesan cheese
salt and ground black pepper
fresh chopped parsley, to serve

Lightly sauté the onion and bacon in half the butter for about 5 minutes, without browning. Add the rice, stir and fry for a minute until opaque. Pour in the stock, stock cube, sugar and seasoning. Bring to the boil then simmer, covered, for about 12 minutes until the rice is just cooked. Add the peas and cook again for 3 minutes. Finally, just before serving, stir in the remaining butter and cheese. Serve as soon as possible. The mixture should be like a thick soup. If necessary, add extra stock, and serve sprinkled with parsley.

FRITTATA

A frittata is something like a pastryless quiche and as such can be eaten hot or cold – it's particularly good for picnics. Basically, it is a firmly cooked omelette with cheese and/or vegetables.

Serves 4

CHOICE OF FILLINGS:

○ 125 g (4 oz) button mushrooms, sliced and sautéd, with 1 tablespoon sautéd chopped onion and ½ sautéd sliced green pepper

○ about 175 g (6 oz) cooked or canned asparagus spears, cut in small lengths

○ 250 g (8 oz) blanched and well-drained leaf spinach with 2 tablespoons grated Gruyère cheese

○ ½ × 400 g can peeled plum tomatoes, well drained, 1 tablespoon fresh chopped basil or parsley and 1 small, sliced onion, sautéd.

FRITTATA MIXTURE:
6 eggs, beaten
1 tablespoon extra virgin olive oil
25 g (1 oz) butter
2–3 tablespoons grated parmesan cheese
salt and ground black pepper

If using a filling, prepare and cook first, then mix it in with the eggs. Season. In a large thick-bottomed frying pan, heat the oil and butter, and when the butter starts to foam, pour in the eggs. Cook on a low heat without disturbing the mixture, (unlike an omelette) for about 12 minutes, until the base is firm and the top slightly runny. Sprinkle over the cheese and flash the pan under a hot grill to just set the top. Slide out onto a warm platter and serve cut into wedges.

5   FISH

The Italians are great fish-eaters, which is not surprising as so much of their country is coastline.

ROAST MONKFISH WITH TOMATO AND CAPER SAUCE

Serves 4

1 kg (2 lb) monkfish tail, central bone removed
1 clove garlic, cut in slivers
small sprigs fresh rosemary or thyme
2–3 tablespoons olive oil

FOR THE *SOFFRITO:*

1 small onion, chopped
2 carrots, chopped
1 stick celery, chopped
50 g (2 oz) mushrooms
25 g (1 oz) butter
3 tablespoons dry vermouth

FOR THE SAUCE:

400 g can chopped tomatoes
1 orange, grated rind and juice
2 tablespoon capers, chopped if large
salt and ground black pepper

OVEN TEMPERATURE: Gas Mark 5/190°C/375°F

A soffrito *is a finely chopped pre-fried vegetable mixture, similar to the French* duxelles.

Preheat the oven. Peel or cut off as much of the light grey membrane on the fish as possible. Lay the fillets on top of each other, to make an oblong parcel, seasoning in between. Tie with kitchen string. Stab the flesh in a few places and insert the garlic slivers and herb sprigs. Sweat the *soffrito* vegetables in the butter in a covered saucepan over a gentle heat for 10 minutes. Uncover and add the vermouth. Bubble up until reduced (about 3 minutes) and season well. Spoon the *soffrito* into a medium-size shallow baking dish, and place the monkfish on top. Brush the fish very well with half the oil, season the top, then bake for about 35–40 minutes, basting twice with the remaining oil. Remove the fish and keep warm.

Add the tomatoes, orange rind and juice to the pan and cook for 5 minutes, and taste for seasoning. To serve the sauce smooth, simply purée, otherwise leave chunky. Stir in the capers and re-heat a little before serving, poured over or around the fish.

BARBECUE MACKEREL WITH BAY AND GARLIC

Serves 4

4 mackerel, about 375 g (12 oz) each, gutted and cleaned
8 large bay leaves
150 ml (¼ pint) olive oil
2 cloves garlic, crushed
juice of 1 lemon
8 large bay leaves
salt and pepper
lemon quarters, to serve

OVEN TEMPERATURE, IF USING: Gas Mark 5/190°C/375°C

Preheat the oven, if using. Slash the mackerel 3 times on each side. Lay a bay leaf in each body cavity and place one on top of each fish. Place in a large shallow dish. Mix the oil, garlic, lemon juice and seasoning and pour over the fish. Cover and marinate for at least 2 hours, turning once and rearranging the bay leaves. Barbecue or grill for about 5 minutes on each side, basting with the marinade. Place the top bay leaves inside the cavity with the other ones.

Alternatively, the fish can be baked for 20–25 minutes, basting once or twice. Serve with wedges of lemon and a green salad.

CRUMBED PRAWNS WITH GREEN SAUCE

Serves 4

16 large uncooked frozen prawns, thawed
3 tablespoons natural dried breadcrumbs
2 tablespoons grated parmesan cheese
½ teaspoon garlic salt
2 tablespoons olive oil
lemon wedges and parsley sprigs, to garnish

FOR THE SAUCE:
1 egg yolk
1 tablespoon capers, chopped finely
2 whole anchovies, finely chopped or 1 teaspoon anchovy essence
2 tablespoons fresh chopped parsley
1 clove garlic, crushed
juice ½ lemon
5 tablespoons olive oil
ground black pepper

Peel the prawns, leaving the tails intact and cutting out the black vein running down the backs. Wash and drain. Put 4 prawns at a time onto skewers, bending them into curves by threading the skewer through both their ends. Mix the breadcrumbs, cheese and garlic salt and sprinkle on both sides of the skewered prawns, pressing down lightly. Chill, uncovered, until ready to cook. Put the egg yolk and remaining sauce ingredients, except the oil, into a food processor or liquidiser and process until smooth, then slowly trickle in the oil. Reserve until serving. Preheat the grill and place the crumbed prawns on the grid. Trickle or brush over 1 of the 2 tablespoons of oil and grill until golden, about 2–3 minutes. Turn over, trickle or brush over the remaining oil and cook the other side. Serve the prawns as soon as possible, garnished with wedges of lemon, sprigs of parsley and a good spoonful of the sauce.

Barbecue Mackerel with Bay and Garlic; Crumbed Prawns with Green Sauce

WHOLE BAKED FISH WITH FENNEL STUFFING

Ideally, use a sea bass for this, which has a superb flavour and texture, or failing that, a salmon or sea trout.

Serves 4–6

1–1.25 kg (2–3 lb) whole fish, gutted and cleaned
1 small bulb fennel, chopped finely
1 small onion, chopped
125 g (4 oz) lean unsmoked bacon, de-rinded and chopped
25 g (1 oz) butter
grated rind and juice of 1 lemon
50 g (2 oz) fresh white breadcrumbs
2 tablespoons fresh chopped parsley
150 ml (¼ pint) dry white wine
salt and ground black pepper
fresh chopped dill, to garnish

OVEN TEMPERATURE: Gas Mark 5/190°C/375°F

Preheat the oven. Pat the fish dry and season well. Sweat the vegetables and bacon in the butter in a covered saucepan on a gentle heat until softened, about 10 minutes. Remove from the heat, add the lemon rind, breadcrumbs, parsley and plenty of seasoning. Spoon into the fish's cavity and press well to enclose. Lay the fish in a large, lightly-greased baking pan, and pour over the lemon juice and wine. Season the top, cover and bake for about 35 minutes or until the fish just flakes when parted from the backbone. Serve the fish on a large platter garnished with dill. Strain the juices into a separate sauce jug. Fillet the fish, and skin it, if you wish, to serve.

PAN-FRIED MULLET WITH A VERMOUTH SAUCE

Red mullet are very popular in Italy and are increasingly easy to find in this country, even though frozen. They keep their pretty colour when cooked and look most appetising served with this tomato and pepper sauce.

Serves 4

4 red mullets, about 250 g (8 oz) each, gutted and cleaned
flour, for dredging
4 tablespoons olive oil
juice of 1 lemon
1 onion, sliced
1 clove garlic, crushed
1 small green pepper, de-seeded and sliced
4 tablespoons dry vermouth
400 g can chopped tomatoes
2 sprigs fresh thyme or 1 teaspoon dried thyme
salt and ground black pepper

Toss the fish in the flour until well coated. Heat 3 tablespoons of oil in a large heavy-based frying pan and fry the mullets for about 5 minutes on both sides until cooked. Season in the pan, remove to a large serving platter, sprinkle with the lemon juice and keep warm, uncovered. Add the remaining oil to the pan and gently fry the onion, garlic and pepper for about 5 minutes. Add the vermouth and cook until reduced by half. Stir in the tomatoes, thyme and seasoning. Bring to the boil then simmer, uncovered for 10 minutes, stirring occasionally. Spoon the sauce down the centre of the fish and serve as soon as possible.

Note: Although not as attractive to look at as red mullets, this recipe also works well with herrings.

Whole Baked Fish with Fennel Stuffing; Pan-fried Mullet with a Vermouth Sauce

FISH WITH PARMESAN CRUMB COATING

Make up a batch of two or three times this tasty, cheese and herb crumb mixture which is ideal not only for fish, but also chicken, veal and pork.

Serves 4

750 g (1½lb) fresh white fish fillets, e.g. haddock, cod or whiting

2 eggs, beaten

corn oil, for deep-frying

lemon wedges, to serve

ground black pepper

fresh parsley or salad leaves, to garnish

FOR THE CRUMB COATING:

125 g (4 oz) dried natural breadcrumbs

8 tablespoons grated parmesan cheese

1 tablespoon paprika

1 tablespoon dried oregano

1 teaspoon dried basil

1 tablespoon garlic salt

2 teaspoons ground bay leaves, if available

Cut the fish into four portions. Mix all the crumb coating ingredients together and place in a shallow bowl. Dip the fish first into the egg then the crumbs – for best results, repeat the coating. Set the fish aside on flat plates. Pour enough oil to fill a deep fat frying pan half-full – no more, for safety's sake. Heat the oil to a temperature of 185°C/375°F or until a cube of day-old bread browns in about half a minute. *Do not leave the pan unattended whilst the heat is on.* Deep-fry the fish in a frying basket, in two batches for about 5 minutes until the coating is golden brown. Drain on kitchen towel. Reheat the oil for the second batch. Keep the first batch warm, uncovered, in a low oven. Serve with wedges of lemon, and garnished with parsley or some green salad leaves.

TROUT COOKED IN PAPER –
Trota in cartoccio

A simple way of baking whole trout, although you may find it easier to use foil instead of paper. Serve each person with a complete parcel so they can open it up and savour the delicious smell for themselves.

Serves 4

4 trout, about 375 g (12 oz) each, gutted and cleaned
2 tablespoons olive oil
1 onion, sliced
1 clove garlic, crushed
125 g (4oz) button mushrooms
150 ml (¼ pint) dry white wine or fish stock
pinch dried thyme
4 tablespoons single cream, optional
salt and ground black pepper

OVEN TEMPERATURE: Gas Mark 5/190°C/375°F

Preheat the oven. Place each fish on a large piece of greaseproof paper or foil, which has been brushed lightly with some oil. Lightly fry the onion and garlic in the remaining oil until softened, about 10 minutes. Chop the mushrooms if any are a little large and add to the pan along with half the wine or stock, the thyme and seasonings. Cook for a further 5 minutes until reduced down. Spoon into the cavities of the trout, and press the sides over to enclose well. Season, draw up the paper or foil and pour over the remaining wine or stock and cream, if using. Completely wrap the fish up, keeping the joins on top to prevent any leakage, and securing with paper clips if necessary. Place on a baking sheet and bake for about 15–20 minutes until cooked.

Serve the parcels as they are and let your guests unwrap them.

6 MEAT AND POULTRY

Although Italians do not eat as much meat as we do in this country, nevertheless they have some delicious poultry and meat recipes in addition to their pasta sauces. Chicken, beef, lamb and veal all feature strongly – often simply brushed with aromatic olive oil and herbs and grilled or quickly fried, flavoured with a little wine, vermouth, tomatoes or herbs. A meat course will often follow a more filling pasta course – so portion sizes are sometimes smaller.

PORK CHOPS WITH SAGE CHEESE COATING

A simple idea that makes chops just a little bit more special and tasty. You could also use lamb chops.

Serves 4

4 pork chops, about 125 g (4 oz) each
1 egg, beaten
125 g (4 oz) natural dried breadcrumbs
2 tablespoons grated parmesan cheese
2 teaspoons dried sage
2–3 tablespoons olive oil
salt and ground black pepper

Trim the chops of rind and fat. Dip in the egg. Mix the crumbs, cheese, sage and seasoning together, then coat the chops well. Heat the oil in a heavy-based frying pan and fry the chops for about 7–10 minutes on each side, making sure the coating does not burn. Remove and drain. Serve with a salad and maybe some home-made tomato sauce (see page 26).

Pork Chops with Sage Cheese Coating; Meatballs with Mozzarella

MEATBALLS WITH MOZZARELLA –
Polpettini e mozzarella

Once you've eaten these very tasty meatballs, you'll never want to make ordinary ones again! Inside is a nugget of creamy cheese, which oozes out when cut open. Serve with the tomato sauce on page 26.

Serves 6–8

500 g (1 lb) lean minced beef
500 g (1 lb) lean minced pork
2 cloves garlic, crushed
grated rind and juice 1 lemon
2 eggs, beaten
2 slices day-old bread, made into crumbs
½ × 80 g drum grated parmesan cheese
½ teaspoon cinnamon
1 teaspoon dried oregano or marjoram
150 g pack mozzarella cheese or bel paese, cut into 16 cubes
about 125 g (4 oz) natural dried breadcrumbs or semolina, to coat
150 ml (¼ pint) olive oil, to fry
2 tablespoons fresh chopped parsley, to serve
salt and ground black pepper

OVEN TEMPERATURE: Gas Mark 4/180°C/350°F

Preheat the oven. Mix the meats, garlic, lemon juice and rind, eggs, fresh breadcrumbs, parmesan cheese, cinnamon, herbs and seasoning. Using wet hands, shape into 16 balls, pressing a cheese cube in the centre of each. Roll in the dried crumbs or semolina. Heat the oil in a large frying-pan and brown the meat balls well, turning carefully. Place in a roasting pan and bake for about 25 minutes until cooked. Serve hot, sprinkled with parsley and accompanied by tomato sauce and pasta.

ROMAN SPICED BRAISED BEEF

Serves 4–6

1 kg (2 lb) lean braising beef, in 3–4 thick slices
2 tablespoons flour
4 tablespoons olive oil
1 large onion
4 cloves
2 cloves garlic, crushed
250 g (8 oz) carrots, peeled and cut in thick chunks
2 sticks celery, cut in thick chunks
300 ml (½ pint) dry red wine
2 tablespoons tomato purée
300 ml (½ pint) stock
125 g (4 oz) peperoni sausage, sliced, or good quality cooked chipolatas, sliced
1 teaspoon ground cinnamon
freshly grated nutmeg
3 bay leaves
2 strips orange peel, pith scraped off
salt and ground black pepper

OVEN TEMPERATURE: Low or Slow

Cut each slice of beef into 4–6 pieces, then toss in flour. Fry in half the oil until browned and remove to a large casserole dish or roasting pan. Cut the onion in quarters. In one quarter stick the four cloves and cut the rest in half again. Add the remaining oil to the pan and sauté the onion, garlic, carrots and celery for 5 minutes. Spoon on top of the beef. Pour the wine into the frying-pan and boil until reduced by half. Sprinkle over any leftover flour and stir in the tomato purée and stock. Bring to the boil, add the remaining ingredients and season well. Pour over the meat and vegetables. Cover first with a large sheet of wet greaseproof paper, then the casserole lid or foil, and cook on the low or slow setting of the oven for at least 6 hours. This can be done overnight in an automatic oven and the dish cooled and re-heated the next day.

Ossobuco; Lamb Fricassee with Egg and Lemon Sauce; Roman Spiced Braised Beef

LAMB FRICASSEE WITH EGG AND LEMON SAUCE

Serves 4–6

1.75 kg (4 lb) leg of lamb, boned and cubed, or
1 kg (2 lb) lamb neck fillets, cubed

2 tablespoons flour

4 tablespoons olive oil

2 fresh or canned artichoke hearts, optional

2 leeks, diced in thick chunks

3 carrots, diced in thick chunks

200 ml (7 fl oz) dry white wine

300 ml (½ pint) chicken or vegetable stock

1 teaspoon juniper berries

1 clove garlic, chopped finely

2 tablespoons fresh chopped parsley

1 teaspoon grated lemon rind

2 egg yolks

juice of ½ lemon

salt and ground black pepper

OVEN TEMPERATURE: Gas Mark 4/180°C/350°F

Preheat the oven. Toss the lamb in the flour to coat. Heat the oil in a frying pan and brown the meat. Remove with a slotted spoon to a casserole. If using fresh artichokes, prepare according to directions on page 22, then slice into strips. Sauté the vegetables in the pan for 5 minutes, then spoon on top of the meat. Pour the wine into the pan and boil until reduced by half, then add the stock and juniper berries. When bubbling, pour into the casserole. Season well, cover and cook in the oven for an hour. Mix together the *gremolada* garnish – the garlic, parsley and lemon rind – and stir it into the casserole. Return to the oven for a further 15 minutes. Beat the yolks and lemon juice, pour into the casserole in a thin stream, stirring vigorously. Do not re-heat; the mixture should thicken slightly. Serve as soon as possible after adding the yolks.

OSSOBUCO

Serves 8

8 veal shank slices about 2 cm (¾ inch) thick, or 8 pork spare rib chops
4 tablespoons flour
4 tablespoons olive oil
1 large onion, sliced
2 carrots, sliced
2 sticks celery, sliced
125 g (4 oz) unsmoked bacon, de-rinded and sliced
300 ml (½ pint) dry white wine
300 ml (½ pint) stock
2 × 400 g cans peeled plum tomatoes
2 sprigs fresh thyme
2 large bay leaves
salt and ground black pepper

FOR THE *GREMOLADA*, TO SERVE:

3 tablespoons fresh chopped parsley
1 clove garlic, chopped
grated rind ½ lemon

OVEN TEMPERATURE: Gas Mark 3/170°C/325°F

Preheat the oven. Using a sharp knife, scrape out the marrow from the bones, if using veal shank slices, and chop. Toss the meat in the flour then fry in the oil until browned. Remove to a large casserole or roasting pan. In the pan juices, sauté the vegetables, chopped marrow and bacon for 5 minutes, then spoon on top of the meat. Add the wine to the pan and boil until reduced by half, then add the stock and tomatoes, squashing the tomatoes roughly. Season well and add the herbs. Pour on top of the vegetables, cover and bake for about 2 hours until the meat is meltingly tender. Mix the *gremolada* ingredients together and add. Return the dish to the oven for a further 10 minutes then serve hot.

Note: This dish, ideal for cooking ahead, improves in flavour if made the day before serving. If you do so, add the *gremolada* after re-heating.

THE DEVIL'S CHICKEN –
Pollo alla Diavola

A great Italian favourite, and ideal for cooking on the barbecue. Young chickens are split in two, marinated in a chilli oil and then grilled until the skin is crispy and the flesh juicy and tender. Make it as hot as you dare!

Serves 4

2 × 1.1 kg (2½ lb) roasting chickens
6 tablespoons extra virgin olive oil
2–4 small dried chillies, crushed
salt and ground black pepper
2 lemons, to serve

Using sharp kitchen scissors, cut the birds through the breast bones and open out. Beat lightly with a rolling pin to flatten slightly. Mix the oil, chilli and a good dessertspoon of ground black pepper. Divide between, and pour into, two polythene bags. Put a bird in each bag and rub the oil well into the flesh. Chill for at least 2 hours, but this could be overnight. To hold the birds flat for cooking, secure diagonally with metal skewers from the legs through to the wings. Sprinkle with salt. Place on a barbecue or a grill pan with a well pre-heated grill, and cook for about 20 minutes, basting occasionally with any leftover oil, turning once. The skin should go slightly blackened and crispy. Check to see the birds are cooked by piercing the thighs. If pink juice runs out, then return to cook further.

Serve sprinkled with fresh lemon juice, with shredded ice cold lettuce and *Bruschetta* bread (page 10).

Devil's Chicken

POT ROAST CHICKEN WITH PARMESAN RICE STUFFING

Serves 4

1.5–1.75 kg (3½–4 lb) roasting chicken
1 onion, chopped
1 small bulb fennel, chopped
4 tablespoons olive oil
125 g (4 oz) long grain or risotto rice, cooked and drained
3 tablespoons grated parmesan cheese
1 egg, beaten
pinch dried oregano
2 tablespoons fresh chopped parsley
3 tablespoons toasted pine kernels or flaked almonds
300 ml (½ pint) chicken stock
3 tablespoons dry vermouth, optional
1 tablespoon cornflour slaked with a little cold water
salt and ground black pepper

OVEN TEMPERATURE: Gas Mark 5/190°C/375°F

Preheat the oven. Untruss the birds if necessary and pull out the pads of fat just inside by the parson's nose. Chop the liver. Reserve the rest of the giblets. Sweat the onion, fennel and liver in half the oil, stirring occasionally, for 10 minutes. Add the rice, parmesan, egg, herbs, nuts and seasonings. Spoon into the body cavity and under the neck skin. Re-truss, or simply tie the legs together firmly over the breast bone. Place in a deep casserole surrounded by the giblets, the stock, vermouth, if using, and more seasoning. Brush the bird well with the remaining oil. Cover and cook for 1 hour, then uncover and return to the oven to brown for a further 20 minutes. Drain the juices off, skim off the fat, then thicken with the cornflour. Allow the bird to stand for 10 minutes before carving. Serve with the juices as a gravy.

CHICKEN CACCIATORE

Translated, this means hunter's chicken; there seems to be a number of different versions. Presumably, whatever ingredients were to hand went into the cooking pot along with the bird. This form of it is a very tasty one and another good 'cook ahead' casserole.

Serves 4

4 chicken quarters or 8 thighs
3 tablespoons flour
4 tablespoons olive oil
1 onion, sliced
2 cloves garlic, crushed
1 green pepper, de-seeded and sliced
75 g (3 oz) unsmoked bacon, de-rinded and chopped
200 ml (7 fl oz) dry white wine, optional
2 × 400 g cans peeled plum tomatoes
250 g (8 oz) button mushrooms, sliced
1 teaspoon dried oregano
2 bay leaves
½ chicken stock cube
125 g (4 oz) large green olives
salt and ground black pepper

Toss the chicken in the flour. Heat the oil and brown the chicken in it. Remove the chicken and set aside. Fry the onion, garlic, pepper and bacon in the remaining pan juices for about 5 minutes, stirring. Add the wine, if using, and boil until reduced by half. Add the tomatoes, squashing roughly, the mushrooms, herbs, stock cube and seasonings. Bring to the boil, return the chicken, cover and simmer gently for about three quarters of an hour, stirring occasionally. Add the olives, simmer again for 5 minutes then adjust the seasoning.

7   SALADS AND VEGETABLES

PEPERONATA

This is a simple salad of sliced, grilled peppers. The addition of a few sultanas gives a traditional sweet/sour balance of flavours, perfect for serving with salty salamis or prosciutto.

Serves 4

2 large red peppers

2 large green peppers

50 g (2 oz) sultanas, optional

FOR THE DRESSING:

3 tablespoons extra virgin olive oil

1 tablespoon wine vinegar or lemon juice

1 clove garlic, crushed

1 teaspoon Dijon mustard

salt and ground black pepper

Grill the peppers under a high heat, turning occasionally until blackened. Cool, peel, de-seed and slice thinly. Put into a shallow serving dish together with the sultanas, if using. Mix all the dressing ingredients together in a jar and pour over. Season. Cover and chill for at least four hours.

Peperonata; Tomato and Bread Salad; Bean and Tuna with Fresh Lemon Dressing

TOMATO AND BREAD SALAD – Panzanella

A simple and absolutely delicious first course. Just as we use soaked bread for soft fruits summer pudding, so the Italians have a classic soaked bread recipe for a salad which is found in many parts of rural Italy. You do need juicy, well-flavoured tomatoes for this, and a good baker's-style uncut loaf, not ready-sliced.

Serves 4–6

4 thick slices baker's-style bread, about 2 days old, white, brown or light rye
½ small onion, preferably red, sliced thinly
500 g (1 lb) ripe tomatoes, preferably large and flavoursome, such as beef or marmande, sliced thinly
½ small green pepper, de-seeded and sliced thinly
125 g (4 oz) mozzarella cheese
1 tablespoon fresh chopped basil or marjoram or 2 tablespoons fresh parsley
about 8 tablespoons extra virgin olive oil
3 tablespoons wine vinegar
juice of ½ lemon
a few pitted black olives, to garnish
salt and ground black pepper

Soak the bread briefly in cold water, immersing completely, then gently squeeze as much water out as possible without breaking the bread up. Soak the onion slices in some cold water for about 10 minutes. Drain. Meanwhile, prepare the other vegetables and slice the cheese in strips. (Mozzarella is easier to cut with a wet knife.) Place the bread in the bottom of a shallow salad dish. On top, layer the tomatoes, peppers, onions and herbs, seasoning well in between, and sprinkling with the oil, vinegar and lemon juice. Arrange slices of cheese and olives on top, cover and chill for at least four hours before serving.

BEAN AND TUNA SALAD WITH FRESH LEMON DRESSING

Serves 4–6

2 × 400 g can white kidney beans or borlotti beans or 1 can of each

200 g (7 oz) can tuna, drained and coarsely flaked

3 spring onions, chopped, or ½ small red onion, sliced thinly

3 tablespoons fresh chopped parsley

1 lemon, grated rind of ½ and juice of whole

3 tablespoons extra virgin olive oil

50 g can anchovies, drain and cut lengthwise

2 eggs, hard-boiled and quartered

salt and ground black pepper

frilly lettuce leaves or large radicchio leaves, to serve

Put everything except the eggs and lettuce leaves into a large bowl. Toss carefully together, seasoning lightly with salt and normally with pepper. Allow to marinate for about 2 hours then pile onto a large serving platter edged with the lettuce or raddichio leaves. Serve lightly chilled and garnished with the egg quarters.

GREEN SALAD WITH CROSTINI

Serves 4–6

A delicious salad can be made by tossing together the following in a large salad bowl, which you can rub with a cut clove of garlic if you like. 1 medium cos or lollo or batavia lettuce, whichever is in season; 1 small bulb of fennel, sliced very thinly; 4 lamb's lettuces; a good handful of rocket leaves or watercress; a good handful of young dandelion leaves; a small head of radicchio; 3–4 spring onions, chopped; 1 carrot, coarsely grated; 2–3 tablespoons of fresh chopped herbs, e.g. basil, marjoram, oregano, parsley; crostini, made with 2–3 slices of bread, from page 15. Just before serving, season very well and dress lightly with: 4 tablespoons of extra virgin olive oil mixd with 1 tablespoon of wine vinegar or lemon juice.

AUBERGINE PARMIGIANA

A classic Italian vegetable dish, suitable as a starter or vegetarian main meal.

Serves 4

3 medium aubergines, sliced
4–6 tablespoons olive oil
500 g (1 lb) mozzarella cheese, sliced
80 g drum grated parmesan cheese

FOR THE SAUCE:

1 large onion, chopped
1–2 cloves garlic, crushed
2 tablespoons olive oil
150 ml (¼ pint) dry red wine, optional
2 × 400 g cans chopped tomatoes with herbs
salt and ground black pepper

OVEN TEMPERATURE: Gas Mark 5/190°C/375°F

Layer the aubergines in a colander, sprinkling in between with salt. Set in a sink to drain for 30 minutes, then rinse well and pat dry with kitchen towel. Preheat the oven. Meanwhile, make the sauce. Lightly fry the onion and garlic in the oil for 5 minutes then add the wine, if using. Boil for 2 minutes then add the tomatoes with herbs, and seasoning. Simmer, uncovered, for 10 minutes. Fry the aubergine in the remaining oil in batches for about 2 minutes on each side until softened, using the oil gradually. Cover the frying pan whilst cooking the aubergines, to cut down on the oil absorption. Drain on kitchen towel. Layer the aubergines, sauce and cheeses finishing with the cheeses. Bake for about 25 minutes until the top is golden brown and bubbling.

Aubergine Parmigiana; Peppers Stuffed with Beans and Rice

PEPPERS STUFFED WITH BEANS AND RICE

Serves 4

4 peppers, green or red, or a mixture
1 onion, chopped
1 clove garlic, crushed
2 small dried chillies, crushed, optional
2 tablespoons olive oil
125 g (4 oz) long grain or risotto rice, cooked and drained
125 g (4 oz) peperoni sausage, or good quality cooked chipolatas, sliced
400 g can red kidney beans, or borlotti beans or white kidney beans, drained
3 tablespoons grated parmesan cheese
2 tablespoons fresh chopped parsley
450 ml (¾ pint) stock
salt and ground black pepper

OVEN TEMPERATURE: Gas Mark 5/190°C/375°F

Preheat the oven. Cut the tops off the peppers and scoop out the seeds. Lightly fry the onion, garlic and chillies, if using, in the oil for about 5 minutes, until softened. Add the rice, sausage, beans, cheese, parsley and seasonings. Cook for a further 3 minutes. Divide between the peppers and replace the tops. Place in a deep casserole and pour in the stock. Cover, without crushing the peppers, and bake for about 45 minutes until the peppers are wrinkled and softened. Serve hot.

RICE, CHICKEN AND SALAMI SALAD

Serves 4

250 g (8 oz) long grain rice, white or brown
125 g (4 oz) whole green beans, tailed and chopped
4 tablespoons extra virgin olive oil
2 tablespoons wine vinegar or lemon juice
2 tomatoes, chopped

7.5 cm (3-inch) length cucumber, diced

2 spring onions, chopped

175 g (6 oz) cooked chicken breast, diced

50 g (2 oz) sliced salami, cut in strips

3 tablespoons fresh chopped mixed herbs or parsley

75 g (3 oz) pitted black olives, halved

salt and ground black pepper

Cook the rice in plenty of salted boiling water, 12 minutes for white rice
and 30–40 minutes for brown. Drain and rinse. Boil the beans for 3–5
minutes until *al dente*, just cooked. Put the rice and beans in a large bowl
and toss in the oil and vinegar. Season and allow to cool. Mix in the rest of
the ingredients when quite cold, adjust the seasoning and serve lightly
chilled.

PEAS WITH LETTUCE

Serves 4–6

150 ml (¼ pint) stock

1 medium cos lettuce, shredded

1 onion, sliced

25 g (1 oz) butter

500 g (1 lb) frozen peas

1 tablespoon fresh chopped marjoram or 1 teaspoon dried marjoram

salt and ground black pepper

Put the stock in a pan with the lettuce, onion and butter. Cover, bring to the
boil, and simmer for 5 minutes. Add the peas, marjoram and seasoning,
return to the boil and simmer for a further 3 minutes. Serve as soon as
possible.

8 DESSERTS

FRUITS AND CHEESES

Normally, a meal in Italy, as in many Mediterranean countries, is rounded off with fresh fruit, and perhaps some cheese. Italy produces some of the best fruits in the world – pears, peaches, grapes, nectarines, melons and cherries to name but a few.

These are often served ready prepared for eating – lightly chilled on a plate, sometimes with a knife and fork. A juicy, quartered pear with a few grapes, and a small chunk of fresh parmesan, pecorino (a ewe's milk cheese), or Gorgonzola is a particularly good ending to a modern Italian meal.

Most Italian cheeses come from the north, ranging from soft and semi-soft types through to hard, well-aged parmesans. As interest grows in this country in continental cheeses, so one sees a greater variety of Italian cheeses not only in Italian delicatessens, but also in larger supermarkets. Dolcelatte, a rare cheese in Britain some years ago, is now quite commonplace, as is bel paese. Pecorino (a tangy ewe's milk cheese) can be used not only in cooking, but also for dessert. Provolone, a smooth, hard cheese can come in a variety of shapes (even shaped like little pigs), but is often sold in large rolls from which slices are cut. Another delicious cheese is mascarpone, from Lombardy, whilst there is a smoked version of mozzarella called provola affumicata which is served sliced. Simply serve with really fresh crusty bread and no butter. It's not necessary!

Fruit and Cheese Italian-style

ZUPPA INGLESE

Believe it or not, this is an Italian trifle! The story goes that Lord Nelson's chef introduced it to an Italian chef, during one of the Mediterranean naval campaigns in the last century. Certainly, the name translated means 'English Soup', and some versions of this dish are almost thin custards. It is very rich and quite sweet, but well worth making for a special dinner party pudding. A little goes a long way.

Serves 6

450 ml (¾ pint) milk
2 dessertspoons flour
175 g (6 oz) caster sugar
1 teaspoon vanilla essence
3 eggs, separated
1 tablespoon chopped angelica
1 tablespoon chopped candied peel
50 g (2 oz) plain chocolate, melted
about 250 g (8 oz) Madeira cake or stale Victoria sponge
3 tablespoons Marsala wine or sweet sherry

OVEN TEMPERATURE: Gas mark 4/180°C/350°F

Preheat the oven. Blend 2 tablespoons of milk with the flour. Scald the rest with 3 tablespoons of sugar and the essence until just on the point of boiling. Stir the hot milk into the flour mixture, blending briskly until thickened. Return to the heat and cook for about a minute. Beat the egg yolks in a bowl and slowly whisk in the thickened milk. Pour half the custard into the base of a clear heatproof dish. Scatter over the candied fruits and leave to cool. Mix the remaining custard with the melted chocolate. Reserve. Cut the cake into pieces, fit it over the plain custard, and scatter over the Marsala or sherry. Leave to soak, then pour over the chocolate custard. Make a meringue by whisking the egg whites until stiff. Slowly whisk in the remaining caster sugar until thick and glossy. If you do not have a very sweet tooth, you can reduce the amount of sugar. Spoon on top of the chocolate layer, swirling attractively, then bake for about 15 minutes until lightly golden. Cool and serve chilled.

LAMBRUSCO AND BLACKCURRANT WATER ICE

Lambrusco is a slightly fizzy medium sweet red wine from northern Italy. It makes a good base for a tangy, fruity sorbet.

Serves 4–6

70 cl bottle frizzante Lambrusco wine
250 g (8 oz) caster sugar
3 sprigs mint, optional, plus extra to garnish
500 g (1 lb) blackcurrants, de-stalked

Heat the wine and dissolve the sugar in it. Bring to the boil, then simmer for 5 minutes with the mint, if using. Add the currants and simmer again for 10 minutes. Cool, purée, and pour into a shallow container. Freeze until nearly solid, then beat well with a whisk or blend in a food processor. Return to the freezer and re-freeze until firm. Cover and store until required. Allow to thaw for about 20 minutes before serving. Garnish with mint.

AMARETTI SEMI FREDDO

Amaretti biscuits are small, crisp, sugary macaroons sold wrapped up in tissue paper, like sweets. If you can't find them, use crumbled macaroons or ratafia biscuits instead.

Serves 8

2 litres of good vanilla dairy ice cream, preferably Italian
20 amaretti biscuits or 5 large macaroons, or 40 ratafias, crushed or crumbled
100 g bar plain chocolate, coarsely grated

Thaw the ice cream slightly and blend in the crushed biscuits and chocolate. Spoon back into the container and re-freeze until firmer but not completely solid. Serve with soft berry fruits like raspberries, strawberries and cherries, or sliced ripe peaches.

Amaretti Semi Freddo; Zuppa Inglese; Lambrusco and Blackcurrant Water Ice

FRESH ORANGE FRUIT SALAD

Serves 4–6

6 large oranges

1 lemon, grated rind and juice

4 tablespoons granulated sugar

150 ml (¼ pint) water

Using a knife or potato peeler, cut about 6 long strips of peel from one of the oranges, and cut into julienne strips. Scrape all the pith off. Squeeze the juice from one orange and reserve. Cut all the peel and pith from the other five fruits. Then slice into thin rounds. Place in a deep fruit bowl. Dissolve the sugar in the water in a saucepan. Bring to the boil, add the julienne strips and simmer for 5 minutes. Cool and add the grated lemon rind and both lemon and orange juices. Pour over the orange slices, cover and chill at least overnight.

ICED COFFEE – Granita di caffe

Serves 3–4

3–4 tablespoons continental roast ground coffee

a small strip of orange peel, optional

2–3 tablespoons sugar

150 ml (¼ pint) whipping cream

Make up 600 ml (1 pint) of strong coffee with the ground coffee, steeping the orange strip in it, if using. Strain, and sweeten with the sugar, to taste. Cool, then pour into a shallow container and freeze. Check every half hour or so, and stir well with a whisk during freezing. A *granita* is best served slighly slushy, so thaw slightly if necessary before spooning into tall glasses. Serve with lightly whipped cream.

INDEX TO RECIPES